CLAIRE CLONINGER

Postcards from Heaven

Courage & Comfort from God's Heart to Yours

New Hope Publishers | Birmingham, Alabama

New Hope Publishers
P. O. Box 12065
Birmingham, AL 35202-2065
www.newhopepublishers.com

Library of Congress Cataloging-in-Publication Data
Cloninger, Claire.
Postcards from heaven : courage and comfort from God's heart to yours / Claire Cloninger.
p. cm.
ISBN 1-56309-843-1 (hardcover)
1.   Consolation. I. Title.
BV4905.3.C56 2004
248.8'6—dc22
2004013345

ISBN: 1-56309-843-1

N044125 • 1004 • 7.5M1

THIS BOOK IS LOVINGLY DEDICATED TO CURTIS,
my firstborn, who sees like a prophet and loves like a servant,
AND TO ANDY, my prodigal, whose faith is a light to the lost.

CON

I Mean It for Good

I Have Glorious Plans for You!

I Want First Place in Your Life

Here's How to Show Your Love

Come, Be Renewed

Someone Understands

Open Your Clenched Fists

Always Be Thankful!

This Is a Job for You

Your Work Is Not My First Concern

Get a Grip! Stand Steady

Speak a Blessing to Someone

Bring Me the Things That Worry You

Why Do You Question My Design?

Come Forth and Live!

Praising Me Can Heal You

Come Away from the Comfortable

You Are a Portrait in Progress

Return to Me

Cry Out to Me

The News Is Good

Now You Belong

The Ending Is Good

Begin in Your Heart

Use What Is Yours!

Thank Me for Trials

Come Believing

Share What You Have Been Given

Introduction

Early in my Christian walk, someone told me that the Bible was a love letter from God to His people. I've never forgotten that. I can hardly think of a crisis in my life, little or large, from that time to this, when I haven't gone to the Word of God for comfort, guidance, and strength. And I've never come away empty-handed.

Many times when I've needed a touch from the Lord, He has led me to a particular verse or passage. Years ago I learned to "personalize" those special messages, to rephrase them as from God's heart directly to me.

For instance, I might personalize a verse like "And my God will supply all your needs according to His riches in glory in Christ Jesus" (Philippians 4:19) like this: "Dear Claire, I am in the process of taking care of your problem. I know exactly what you need, and I intend to supply that need from My glorious storehouse of riches in Christ Jesus. Your loving Father, God."

I began to think of these "personalized" Scripture verses as "postcards from heaven." What power they have had over the years to alter my attitude and increase my faith!

Several summers ago, while I was attending a church conference in the mountains of North Carolina, the Lord led me to send one of these "postcards from heaven" to my friend Toni, who was going through a tough time. It was then that I discovered their power to minister to others.

From childhood, Toni's life had been a series of losses and tragedies. Although she was happily married to a wonderful man, there were places of pain in her past that she had never dealt with. The result? At some subconscious level, Toni was furious at God. But being a "good Christian," she was having trouble acknowledging that, even to herself.

It was during one of the conference workshops on inner healing that Toni began to recognize her anger. She stayed after the teaching to confer with the workshop leader, a wise young pastor who suggested that Toni go back to her cabin and spend as much time as she needed writing a very honest letter to God. He assured her that God already knew her true feelings but that He wanted her to be willing to acknowledge and express them herself. "God prefers your honest anger to a veneer of false acceptance any day," the workshop leader told Toni.

Toni wrote the letter. In the heart-wrenchingly honest words of a wounded child, she poured out the pain of a lifetime. She released her feelings of abandonment and let her anger rage. She pleaded with God to help her understand all that she had been through so that she could accept it and go on. Then she delivered the letter, not to the gates of heaven, but to my cabin!

"Would you be God for me?" she asked me timidly. "I feel like I'm writing into a vacuum. I mean, I know He's there, but it would help me to have somebody read the letter and let me know it's okay."

I read that letter and I wept. Then I prayed.

"Lord," I asked, "what can I say to Toni? Help me tell her that You love her. Help me show her how You feel toward her. Show me what You would say to her, Lord, if You were here in person to take her in Your arms and comfort her."

Suddenly a flood of Scripture began to flow into my mind. Verses of wisdom and comfort and courage began to surface. It was as though the Lord was reminding me of all the words He had already spoken to Toni (and all the Tonis who have ever been wounded by the world). This is the "postcard from heaven" that the Lord led me to write to my friend:

Dear Toni,
I got your letter. I read every word, and I understand. There are so many things I want you to know. You are My child—precious to Me. When you are hurting, I hurt, too. When this fallen and imperfect world wounds one of My children, I am wounded, too.

DO YOU KNOW THAT I AM RIGHT HERE BESIDE YOU? I always have been, and I always will be. I will not leave you comfortless. When you walk through the dark valley, I will be with you. You must open your eyes of faith and use them to see Me in the midst of your situation. I am here, and I'm on your side. I want you to keep talking to Me. Cast every care of your heart upon Me, because I care for you. Do not give way to panic. I will keep your heart and mind in perfect peace. Walk with Me. Let Me be your God. Your husband cannot be your God. Neither can your friends. I have given you these special people to care for you and help you. But no human being can ever be to you who I am. I am your God. Let Me prove myself to you. You are My own.

Your Father for all time,
God

In a magnificent mountain setting, Toni read her "postcard from heaven." Only she and God know exactly what happened as she read. But she later confided to me that a new phase of trust and communication began that day between herself and God. She said that though the words she read hadn't answered all of her questions, they had showed her the Father-heart of God. And that was the beginning of healing in her relationship with Him.

I know that the words of the "postcard" had power in Toni's situation because they were from God's heart. Each attitude and emotion expressed on God's behalf is directly traceable to His character as revealed in the Bible. The Scriptures for Toni's "postcard" are Ephesians 1:17-21; Philippians 4:6-7; Matthew 11:28-30; Deuteronomy 33:27; Jeremiah 29:11-13; Jeremiah 31:3; Romans 8:31-39; John 14:1, 18, 27; and Hebrews 13:8.

God is trying to communicate with each of us every day in every situation of our lives. His care and concern for every one of our problems is personal and individual. The Holy Spirit is longing to minister the good news of God's Word to every pain, need, concern, or area of confusion in our lives. (It's no accident that Jesus urged us to pray to God as Abba—the Hebrew equivalent of "Daddy.")

Not only are these messages wonderful to receive into our own lives, they are also wonderful to share with others who are needing a word from God. As you read, you may find a particular "postcard" that would encourage your sister or your neighbor or your child. That is when you will discover, as I did, a joyful new way of giving away God's good news!

—Claire

I Am Doing Something New!

Do not remember the past events,
pay no attention to things of old.
Look, I am about to do something new;
even now it is coming. Do you not see it?
Indeed, I will make a way in the wilderness,
rivers in the desert.
—Isaiah 43:18-19

Dear Child of Mine,

I am the God of new beginnings, of perpetual tomorrows, of new sunsets and sunrises and seasons. With Me the rivers run, the waves constantly cascade onto the shore, the forests that looked dead and life-less leaf out in springtime green, and flowers of every color bloom.

DO NOT DWELL ON YOUR FAILURES, MY CHILD. Everyone has seasons of failure. It's part of being alive. But just because you have failed doesn't mean that you must stay there. Look! I am about to do something new! Even now it is coming: do you not see it? I am making a way, an incredible way in the wilderness of your life. Believe it. I am making rivers in the desert of your yesterday. Trust Me. This is what I am best at doing. This is what I delight to do for My children. Forget the former things. Do not dwell on the past. Move forward with Me.

Your Father,
God

I Made You for a Reason

The word of the LORD came to me:

I chose you before I formed you in the womb;

I set you apart before you were born.

I appointed you a prophet to the nations.

—Jeremiah 1:4-5

For it was You who created my inward parts;

You knit me together in my mother's womb.

I will praise You, because I have been remarkably and wonderfully made.

Your works are wonderful, and I know this very well.

—Psalm 139:13-14

My Dear Child,

I created you for a purpose. There is a specific reason for your life. You are important to Me. When circumstances or people in your life make you feel insignificant, remember that you are of great value and significance to Me. I knew who you would be before you were even born. While you were still in the womb, I was putting you together according to My own design. I formed you exactly as you are.

Don't you see? I DIDN'T MAKE ANY MISTAKES WHEN I MADE YOU. You are wonderfully made! I am filled with pride over you, My precious one! Be at peace with yourself. I love you as you are.

You are you. You are Mine!

Love,
God

I WILL WAIT FOR YOU

So he got up and went to his father. But while the son was still a long way off,
his father saw him and was filled with compassion. He ran, threw his arms around his neck,
and kissed him. The son said to him, "Father, I have sinned against heaven and in your sight.
I'm no longer worthy to be called your son."
But the father told his slaves, "Quick! Bring out the best robe and put it on him;
put a ring on his finger and sandals on his feet. Then bring the fattened calf and slaughter it,
and let's celebrate with a feast, because this son of mine was dead and is alive again;
he was lost and is found!" So they began to celebrate.

—Luke 15:20-24

My Child,

You think you understand My love. But I wonder. Do you know just how much I love to be with you? Do you know how much I miss you when you're gone? You can turn your back on Me and walk away; I'll wait for you. You can move to a foreign country; I'll watch the road for your return. You can ignore My wishes and wander from My ways. You can make the wrong choices and listen to the wrong voices and waste every treasure I've placed in your hands. Still My ear will listen for your knock on the door.

Is it you? I will wonder, and My heart will leap. Is it My child at last? And on that day when I see you from a long way off, weary and broken and headed for home, I will rush out to meet you. I'll cover your shame with a cloak of righteousness. I'll cook a meal and call My friends and plan a celebration. And as I look into your face, which is so dear to Me, tears will fill My eyes, and I will say, "My child was lost, but now is found! MY CHILD WAS DEAD, BUT NOW IS ALIVE AGAIN!"

With open arms!
God

I Am the One You Need

No one will be able to stand against you as long as you live.

I will be with you, just as I was with Moses.

I will not leave you or forsake you.

—Joshua 1:5

I—I am the One who comforts you.

Who are you that you should fear man who dies,

or a son of man who is given up like grass?

—Isaiah 51:12

Dear Child,

Haven't you learned by now where your comfort comes from? Haven't you discovered the wellspring of your joy and the source of your strength? I AM THE GOD WHO COMFORTS YOU. I AM THE FRIEND WHO BRINGS JOY.

Why do you continue to look to the people in your life for things that can only come from Me? I have given you special people to enjoy, care about, learn from, and nurture. But these are human beings like yourself. There will come a time when they will let you down. If you continue to go to them for the fulfillment that can only be found in Me, a time will come when you are left empty and alone.

My love is higher love. It is a love you can trust. I will not leave you nor forget you.

Total fulfillment will not come from others. Being totally "full-filled" means being filled full of My Spirit. Come and be fulfilled in Me.

Your Father and your friend,
God

THERE'S NO NEED TO GO ON LIKE THIS

I planted you, a choice vine from the very best seed.

How then could you turn into a degenerate, foreign vine?

—Jeremiah 2:21

I am the vine; you are the branches. The one who remains in Me and I in him

produces much fruit, because you can do nothing without Me.

If anyone does not remain in Me, he is thrown aside like a branch and he withers.

They gather them, throw them into the fire, and they are burned. If you remain in Me

and My words remain in you, ask whatever you want and it will be done for you.

—John 15:5-7

Dearest Child,

It breaks My heart to see the way you struggle and struggle in your own strength. So often you feel depleted. You push and fret and end up feeling burned out and alone. There is no need for you to go on like this. I long to give you inner strength. Draw on My resources and live as you were designed to live—as a branch attached to the vine of My eternal love. ALL THAT YOU REQUIRE WILL FLOW FROM MY ABUNDANCE TO YOUR NEED. And when My life has filled your emptiness to overflowing, it will branch out into the lives of those around you. I am the vine; you are the branch. Come to Me and live.

Abundantly yours,
God

I AM HERE FOR YOUR HURT

He will not break a bruised reed,

and He will not put out a smoldering wick,

until He has led justice to victory.

—Matthew 12:20

But when He heard this, He said,

"Those who are well don't need a doctor, but the sick do."

—Matthew 9:12

DON'T GIVE UP!

Therefore we do not give up; even though our outer person is being destroyed,

our inner person is being renewed day by day.

For our momentary light affliction is producing for us

an absolutely incomparable eternal weight of glory.

So we do not focus on what is seen, but on what is unseen;

for what is seen is temporary, but what is unseen is eternal.

—2 Corinthians 4:16-18

My Dear Child,

Are you hurting today? Under all the coping mechanisms you've set up to keep your life in motion, is there a place in you that is bruised and aching, a hidden place in need of healing?

I KNOW. I CAN SEE. I WANT TO HEAL YOU. It is to the downtrodden and the broken that I come. Let Me in. Don't hide the wounded places. Don't show Me only the shiny achievements and the competent areas of your life. I am here for the hurt in you, too. I want to bring health to every part of you. I want to see you flourish. I want to make you whole. So when the wick of your candle is smoldering and almost out, cry out to Me. I will send the gentle wind of My Holy Spirit to stir up that flame of life in you.

Compassionately yours,
God

Dear Child,

DO NOT GIVE UP. Do not feel defeated or hopeless or down on yourself. It's true that the outward circumstances of what is happening look grim to you. It's true that the world feels dreary and dismal tonight, and you feel tired. But don't dwell on the outward things, on your physical surroundings or the particulars of this situation. These outward things are actually in the process of deteriorating and passing away right before your eyes.

Your lifetime on this planet only lasts a moment. But you yourself are eternal. You are forever because your real life is in Me and I am in you. Your body may be aging, but your spirit is "youthening"! As you dwell in Me, your spirit person is being vitalized and energized and given new vision.

All the piddling trivia you're wrestling with is but a blink of My eye. All the difficulties and heartaches you're struggling with are already in the process of being formed by My hand into a glory that is beyond your comprehension——a glory that is eternal. So don't keep your eyes glued to the frustrations or the heartaches; lift your eyes to Me. I am more real than anything your eyes can see. I am more powerful than anything your hands can touch. I am more lasting than anything your senses can perceive.

I am real life!
God

YOU CANNOT CHANGE MY LOVE

Love consists in this: not that we loved God, but that He loved us
and sent His Son to be the propitiation for our sins.
—1 John 4:10

But God proves His own love for us in that while we were still sinners Christ died for us!
—Romans 5:8

For by grace you are saved through faith, and this is not from yourselves;
it is God's gift—not from works, so that no one can boast.
—Ephesians 2:8-9

Dear Child of Mine,

As you grew up in this imperfect world, you learned that if you were a good little child, you would be loved. This is called "conditional love" because it comes with conditions——with strings attached. It is love you must struggle to earn. But is not real love. It is counterfeit——a cheap forgery of a priceless masterpiece.

MY LOVE IS REAL AND UNCONDITIONAL. It cannot be earned. Try to understand this truth, for it will deeply affect the way you live your life: You cannot make Me love you more by anything you do or do not do. And you cannot make Me love you less by anything you do or do not do.

Read those two sentences again. If you allow My deep, true love to seep down into your wounded spirit, it will make you whole. And from that endless stream of love I put within you, true repentance will flow. Then you will live a good life, not to make Me love you, but because I already do love you! You will be set free to live with joy and abandon. You will be released to love others with this same kind of love.

Does it sound to good to be true? Dare to believe it. You will never be the same.

Unconditionally,
God

WHAT IS YOUR ANSWER?

"But you," He asked them again, "who do you say that I am?"

Peter answered Him, "You are the Messiah!"

—Mark 8:29

My Child,

There is one question that you alone can answer. When it is put to you, answer carefully. Your reply must flow from the innermost depths of who you are. No authority on earth can help you answer, and no authority on earth can refute your true response. Your answer to this one question will determine the way you live your life. It will mold your character and chart your course. It will be both your anchor and your compass. And it will move for you the very gates of eternity.

"Who do you say I am?" Jesus asked Peter. When that question is put to you, I pray your reply will be, "THE CHRIST, THE SON OF THE LIVING GOD. MY LORD AND MY KING."

Be ready to answer.
God

THE GIFT OF WAITING ON ME

I wait for the Lord; I wait,
and put my hope in His word.
—Psalm 130:5

My Child,

You live in such a hurried world. No one sees the value in waiting. Most people feel that in a doctor's waiting room, for instance, they are doing little more that wasting time. They don't know how to use those precious times of inactivity. Times of inactivity can be a gift when you lift your heart to Me.

IF YOU LET ME, MY CHILD, I WILL TEACH YOU THE VALUE OF WAITING. I will teach you that waiting can be the soil of faith in which your spirit can grow. In the silence of waiting you will become familiar with the still, small voice of My love speaking in your heart. As you do so, you will learn not to rush ahead, acting on your own instincts, but to discern the leading of My Holy Spirit at every small crossroads on your journey. Even when I'm silent, I will teach you to wait for My love to speak, believing that I am with you. Soon you will find yourself looking forward to our special time of quiet. I have so much to say to you.

The One Who Speaks,
God

I Delight in the Ordinary

Your beauty should not consist of outward things like elaborate hairstyles
and the wearing of gold ornaments or fine clothes; instead, it should consist
of the hidden person of the heart with the imperishable quality of a gentle
and quiet spirit, which is very valuable in God's eyes.

—1 Peter 3:3-4

Whatever you do, do it enthusiastically, as something done for the Lord
and not for men, knowing that you will receive the reward
of an inheritance from the Lord—you serve the Lord Christ.

—Colossians 3:23-24

Dear Child,

You look for great ways to bring Me glory. You feel frustrated and somehow stuck in the ordinary things of life. Know this: I delight in the ordinary. I delight in a life lived simply and obediently before Me.

WHEN YOU CHOOSE TO EMBRACE THE SMALL STRUGGLES AND SIMPLE PLEASURES OF THIS ONE DAY, YOU HONOR ME. You cannot offer higher praise to Me than the praise of a calm and joyous life. Do each small task as an offering to Me, for I see and appreciate your work. Enter into each conversation with a determination to let My words come out through you, for I hear and delight in such conversation. In this way, the most common life becomes extraordinary. The simplest day becomes holy.

I am with you in this ordinary day.
God

LEAN INTO MY MERCY

"Do not be afraid, for you will not be put to shame;
don't be humiliated, for you will not be disgraced.
For you will forget the shame of your youth,
and you will no longer remember the disgrace of your widowhood.
For your husband is your Maker—His name is Yahweh of Hosts—
and the Holy One of Israel is your Redeemer;
He is called the God of all the earth.
For the LORD has called you, like a wife deserted and wounded in spirit,
a wife of one's youth when she is rejected," says your God.

—Isaiah 54:4-6

My Dear & Precious Child,

Do you know that when you weep, I am weeping with you? Do you know that your wounds wound Me and your heartaches break My heart?

DO NOT BE AFRAID. YOU ARE NOT ALONE; I AM HERE. Do not fear disgrace, for I will stand up for you in your humiliation. Whatever pain or shame or reproach you have felt in your life, I desire to redeem it and make it right.

I am your God. The Lord Almighty is My name. I am the Holy One of Israel, your Redeemer. Confide in Me, lean into My mercy, trust the strong arm of My righteousness. I will stand up for you.

Mightily and mercifully yours,
God

I Will Do It

Now may the God of peace Himself sanctify you completely.
And may your spirit, soul, and body be kept sound and blameless
for the coming of our Lord Jesus Christ.
He who calls you is faithful, who also will do it.
—1 Thessalonians 5:23-24

My Dear One,

You spend tremendous energy on trying to be a good Christian. But self-effort will never produce the completed saint. Instead, spend that same amount of time and effort just sitting at My feet. READ MY WORD. LISTEN TO MY VOICE. ABSORB MY TRUTH. Let the lifeblood of My gospel begin to flow through your veins, and you will begin to be remade. A person will most surely become like those with whom he or she keeps company. Trust Me. I am faithful, and I will never ask of you what I am not willing to perform in your life.

I will do it!
God

I Am Always There

Where can I go to escape Your Spirit?
Where can I flee from Your presence?
If I go up to heaven, You are there;
if I make my bed in Sheol, You are there.
If I live at the eastern horizon or settle at the western limits,
even there Your hand will lead me; Your right hand will hold on to me.
If I say, "Surely the darkness will hide me,
and the light around me will become night"—
even the darkness is not dark to You.
The night shines like the day; darkness and light are alike to You.

—Psalm 139:7-12

Dear One,

Your life is filled with so many things——so many people and plans and places and appointments. You rise early, and you go to bed late. And though you may stop and turn to Me briefly, in only a moment you are off again into your own thoughts and imaginations and pursuits.

Do you think that I am part of one world and not of another? Do you think that I am the God of prayers and church and not the God of business and relationships? Don't you know that there is no place you can go apart from My Spirit——that My presence goes with you always?

If you go up to heaven, I am there. If you sink to the depths, I am there also. If you fly to the far side of the ocean, I am still there. There is no darkness so deep that My light cannot penetrate and dispel it.

I long for the time when you will welcome Me into every boardroom and living room, every conference and conversation. I WANT TO BE YOUR CONFIDANT. I WANT TO BE YOUR CLOSEST FRIEND.

I want to be your
God

YOUR SOUL WILL DELIGHT IN ABUNDANCE

Come, everyone who is thirsty, come to the waters;
and you without money, come, buy, and eat!
Come, buy wine and milk
without money and without cost!
Why do you spend money on what is not food,
and your wages on what does not satisfy?
Listen carefully to Me, and eat what is good,
and you will enjoy the choicest of foods.

—Isaiah 55:1-2

Dear Child of My Heart,

Do you sometimes feel caught on a treadmill? You wake and you work and you worry. You stop and you sleep and you start all over again. Are you following dreams that are not My dreams and plans that are not My plans? Why do you spend your money on obsessions that only make you restless for more? Why spend your energy on things that will never satisfy that inner hunger in you? I created you with a longing that only I can fill. "Come, everyone who is thirsty, come to the waters; and you without money, come, buy, and eat!"

LISTEN TO ME, TRUST IN ME, REACH OUT TO ME, and your soul will delight in the richness of spiritual abundance.

Your own
God

I Am Drawing Good from Bad

We know that all things work together for the good of those who love God:
those who are called according to His purpose.

—Romans 8:28

Dearest Child,

Everything in your life can be used as a part of My plan for good. Yes, even the bad things. Even the very situation that you think is intolerable or hopeless or unredeemable. Trust Me. This thing, too, will work together for your good and My glory.

How is that possible? It is possible because you love Me, because you have been called to walk in My ways, and you have answered yes to that call. Even now I am in the process of drawing good from the bad. I am committed to taking whatever evil comes into your life and bringing good out of it.

ALL THINGS WILL WORK TOGETHER FOR GOOD. NOT JUST SOME, BUT ALL. Even your own failures and faults and areas of sin are opportunities for Me to work. Commit them to Me. Confess them. Put them under the blood of My Son. Even these things will give you cause to praise Me.

Trust Me in this.
God

Do Not Fall in Love with the World

Do not love the world or the things that belong to the world.

If anyone loves the world, love for the Father is not in him.

Because everything that belongs to the world—the lust of the flesh, the lust of the eyes,

and the pride in one's lifestyle—is not from the Father, but is from the world.

And the world with its lust is passing away, but the one who does God's will remains forever.

—1 John 2:15-17

But the fruit if the Spirit is love, joy, peace, patience, kindness, goodness,

faith, gentleness, self-control. Against such things there is no law.

—Galatians 5:22-23

I call heaven and earth as witnesses against you today

that I have set before you life and death, blessing and curse.

Choose life so that you and your descendants may live.

—Deuteronomy 30:19

My Dearest Child,

The world holds out to you a surface sort of happiness that depends on favorable circumstances. But I hold out joy. The world offers relationships fraught with hidden agendas and self-serving motives. I offer love, gracious and unconditional.

The world holds out blame and shame and condemnation. I hold out forgiveness and the road to a new beginning. The world rewards you with addictions and compulsions and momentary gratification. But I will fill you with peace that passes understanding. The world offers broken contracts, vows, and promises. I give you My Word, which never changes. The world runs hot and cold. One day you're valued and respected; the next you're forgotten like yesterday's headlines. But My character is love, and I am the same yesterday, today, and forever.

Oh, My child, do not fall in love with the world. It holds out to you only an imitation of life. I HOLD OUT LIFE, ABUNDANT AND FREE.

Choose life!
God

LEAVE TOMORROW IN MY HANDS

So don't worry, saying, "What will we eat?" or "What will we drink?" or "What will we wear?"
For the idolaters eagerly seek all these things, and your heavenly Father knows that you need them.
But seek first the kingdom of God and His righteousness, and all these things will be provided for you.
Therefore don't worry about tomorrow, because tomorrow will
worry about itself. Each day has enough trouble of its own.
—Matthew 6:31-34

Dearest Child,

There are two ways you can go about the business of your life. You can be stressed and anxious and crippled with worries. Or you can trust that I am in control, working in your circumstances, and you can be free!

Why is trust so difficult for you? Why do you worry about menus and calories and grams of fat? Why do you fret about styles and fashions and pulling together the right wardrobe? Life is so much more than food. Your body is so much more important than the clothes you put on it every morning.

Look up. See the birds? They have never made a grocery list or counted a calorie, and yet they are fed. Find a field filled with flowers. Spend an hour gazing at their beauty. Do you think they are worried about what's in style this year or what color goes with what? Now, if I take care of birds and flowers, can't you believe that I will take care of you? It is the godless person who worries about these things. But you are My own child. Seek My kingdom, and I'll provide for you. LEAVE TOMORROW IN MY HANDS.

I love you.
God

I'll Give You the Right Words

The LORD said to him, "Who made the human mouth?
Who makes him mute or deaf, seeing or blind? Is it not I, the LORD?"

—Exodus 4:11

Whenever they bring you before synagogues and rulers and authorities,
don't worry about how you should defend yourselves or what you should say.
For the Holy Spirit will teach you at that very hour what must be said.

—Luke 12:11-12

My Own Child,

Trust Me today for the words you need to say. Rely on Me, and I will supply you with the right words for every situation. Dwell in Me, and I will dwell in you. Dwell in the wisdom of My Word, and My wisdom will dwell in you.

Then, when you are called upon to speak, you will know what to say. The words will come from your heart—words of comfort or words of confrontation, whatever you need. Whatever situation arises, you will be able to go to the well of My wisdom and draw from the living water of My Word.

BE BOLD! I AM WITH YOU, NOW AND ALWAYS.

Your strength and supply,
God

I Want to Tell You a Secret

Be careful not to practice your righteousness in front of people, to be seen by them.

Otherwise, you will have no reward from your Father in heaven.

So whenever you give to the poor, don't sound a trumpet before you,

as the hypocrites do in the synagogues and on the streets, to be applauded by people.

I assure you: They've got their reward!

But when you give to the poor, don't let your left hand know what your right hand is doing,

so that your giving may be in secret.

And your Father who sees in secret will reward you.

—Matthew 6:1-4

Dearest Child,

I want to tell you a secret. I want to show you a path of joy. I want to open a door for you that leads to blessing. The key to that door is marked "giving." And not merely "giving," but "giving without expecting any reward or praise from people."

When you give secretly to others without expecting them to reward you, I WILL REWARD YOU WITH A QUIET INNER JOY. When you do your good deeds, expecting no fanfare from people, there will be great fanfare for you in heaven.

Trust Me, My child. Think today of some need that you can meet in secret. Then go about meeting that need in a quiet and thankful way. I will be with you. And we will rejoice together!

Generously,
God

I AM CLOSER THAN YOUR HEARTBEAT

Peace I leave with you. My peace I give to you.
I do not give to you as the world gives.
Your heart must not be troubled or fearful.
—John 14:27

Stop ... and know that I am God.
—Psalm 46:10

My Dearest Child,

I AM CALLING YOU INTO A PLACE OF REST, INTO A HAVEN OF STILLNESS. The world can be a tyrant, pushing and rushing and driving you. You need not yield to its merciless rhythms. I will give to you a peace that the world cannot give or comprehend. I will place My peace within you. I will draw you to Me out of the rush and confusion and will teach you to enter My rest.

Though the world swirls about you like a mad whirlpool, My Spirit at the center of your being is a fountain of stillness and peace. There, I am closer than your heartbeat. There, you can stop and know that I am God.

Enter My rest. There you will know Me.

I am . . .
God

CONSIDER THE GIFTS

For who makes you so superior? What do you have that you didn't receive?
If, in fact, you did receive it, why do you boast as if you hadn't received it?
—1 Corinthians 4:7

For though they knew God, they did not glorify Him as God or show gratitude.
Instead, their thinking became nonsense, and their senseless minds were darkened.
Claiming to be wise, they became fools . . . .
They exchanged the truth of God for a lie, and worshiped and served something
created instead of the Creator, who is blessed forever. Amen.
—Romans 1:21-22, 25

Dearest Child,

Today as you go about your work, consider the gifts you have been given. Think of the talents and abilities I have formed in you that enable you to do your job.

You may say to yourself, "I have been trained or educated to do these things." But think about it. Where did you get the intelligence with which you reason and learn, the talent with which you create, the reflexes that allow you to develop skills? You could not have been educated without these gifts.

It is tempting at times to allow your work to become a subtle kind of idol in your life. Remember when you are in the midst of toiling, laboring, creating, and earning that I, the Lord your God, am a jealous God. Do not worship the work of your hands, but WORSHIP THE ONE WHO HAS EQUIPPED YOU TO DO THE WORK.

Sovereignly,
God

WHEN YOU FALL SHORT

For all have sinned and fall short of the glory of God.

—Romans 3:23

When they heard this, they left one by one, starting with the older men.
Only He was left, with the woman in the center.
When Jesus stood up, He said to her, "Woman, where are they?
Has no one condemned you?"
"No one, Lord," she answered.
"Neither do I condemn you," said Jesus.
"Go, and from now on do not sin any more."

—John 8:9-11

Dear Child,

When you have sinned and fallen short of My glory, believe Me, you are in the company of great Christians everywhere! "All have sinned and fall short" of My glory—there are no exceptions. I know how devastating sin can be to everyone it touches. That is why I sent My perfect Son into the world as an offering for sin. WHEN YOU HAVE FALLEN SHORT, LOOK TO JESUS.

How did He deal with the fallen men and women of his day? Once a woman caught in adultery was brought before Him. He heard her accusers, who wanted to stone her. And the first thing He did was get rid of them! (If Satan has become your accuser, trying to destroy you, speak out the name and the truth of Jesus, and he must back off! Remind him of Calvary and the empty tomb. Remind him whose heel is now upon his head! That should shut him up!)

After getting rid of this woman's accusers, Jesus lifted her to her feet and spoke to her words of affirmation and healing. Then He lovingly sent her off, telling her to sin no more. In short, He restored her. And that is what He wishes to do for you. Don't remain in the devastating aftermath of your sin. Go to Jesus now.

Lovingly,
God

DON'T LOOK BACK

Not that I have already reached the goal or am already fully mature,

but I make every effort to take hold of it

because I also have been taken hold of by Christ Jesus.

Brothers, I do not consider myself to have taken hold of it. But one thing I do:

forgetting what is behind and reaching forward to what is ahead,

I pursue as my goal the prize promised by God's heavenly call in Christ Jesus.

—Philippians 3:12-14

Child of Mine,

THIS JOURNEY WE ARE ON TOGETHER IS FORWARD-LOOKING. The destination is ever before you. You have not arrived, but you are on your way. Press on. Take hold of that glorious purpose for which Jesus Christ has taken hold of you. My purpose is that you know Him, that you become like Him, that your life become a channel through which His love can flow to others.

Many have traveled this road before you, and you can learn from them. Consider Paul. He could have looked back and become paralyzed by the guilt and shame of a life spent persecuting the church of Jesus Christ. Why, Paul even held the coats of the murderers who stoned My servant Stephen! He stood by watching in approval. But once he was forgiven, Paul did not waste time or spiritual energy looking back. He knew that the past had been put under the blood of Jesus, and he was free to press on toward the goal.

Do you know these things about your past? Come be forgiven, once and for all, and then look back no more. Instead, look ahead to the glory that lies out before you.

And press on!
God

BE STRONG IN ME

Finally, be strengthened by the Lord and His vast strength.
Put on the full armor of God so that you can stand against the tactics of the Devil.
For our battle is not against flesh and blood, but against the rulers, against the authorities,
against the world powers of this darkness, against the spiritual forces of evil in the heavens.
This is why you must take up the full armor of God, so that you may be able to resist
in the evil day, and having prepared everything, to take your stand.

—Ephesians 6:10-13

For God has not given us a spirit of fearfulness,
but one of power, love, and sound judgment.

—2 Timothy 1:7

Dearest Child,

There's a battle raging all around you this very day. You cannot see the enemy with your human eyes, for this fight is in the spirit realm, against forces of evil. The enemy soldiers take their orders from the Prince of Darkness, the unseen power who controls this world.

Does all this sound like some sort of a scary story made up to frighten you? Believe Me, it is not; these things are real. You need to be warned. But you do not need to be afraid. Not ever. I have not given you a spirit of fear, but a spirit of power and love and sound judgment. I have provided for your defense and your protection. I am even sending you out as a warrior to stand against this enemy of Mine.

No longer are you to be weak and ineffective. Instead, be strong! Your strength will not come from yourself, but from Me. I have boundless resources of power. So put on My full suit of spiritual armor, and you will surely be able to resist the enemy and to stand for Me through every trial and temptation.

Your Commander-in-Chief,
God

YOU WILL FIND ME

Keep asking, and it will be given to you. Keep searching, and you will find. Keep knocking, and the door will be opened to you. For everyone who asks receives, and the one who searches finds, and to the one who knocks, the door will be opened.

—Matthew 7:7-8

You will seek Me and find Me when you search for Me with all your heart.

—Jeremiah 29:13

God replied to Moses, "I AM WHO I AM. This is what you are to say to the Israelites: I AM has sent me to you."

—Exodus 3:14

Dear Child,

I am not difficult to find. I am not trying to elude you or hide Myself from you. I am here, and when you are ready to find Me, you will. You will find Me when you seek Me with all that you are. When you are through playing intellectual games and spiritual hide-and-seek. When you stop trying to create Me in your image. When you stop giving Me ultimatums and deadlines and telling Me how God should act.

When it's really Me that you want and not some deity of your own design, then you will surely find Me. My name is I AM—the God of power and majesty, the God of justice and mercy. I am Jehovah—the God of the garden, the flood, the wilderness, and the mountaintop. I am Abba—the God of Jesus, the God of the cross and the grave, the Resurrection and the Life. Seek Me; you will find Me.

I AM WHO I AM.
God

TURN AROUND ... NOW

You are of your father the Devil, and you want to carry out your father's desires.
He was a murderer from the beginning and has not stood in the truth,
because there is no truth in him. When he tells a lie, he speaks from his own nature,
because he is a liar and the father of liars.

—John 8:44

My little children, I am writing you these things so that you may not sin.
But if anyone does sin, we have an advocate with the Father—
Jesus Christ the righteous One. He Himself is the propitiation for our sins,
and not only for ours, but also for those of the whole world.

—1 John 2:1-2

Repent, because the kingdom of heaven has come near!

—Matthew 3:2

Dear Child,

So you've slipped and somehow fallen back from your commitment to Me. And now the enemy is trying to tell you that you're really not a Christian, that you'll never make it and you might as well give up. But consider the source. Satan is a liar. He would love to see your life bounce right back into his court.

Would it interest you to know what I think of your situation? Would it surprise you to know that your sin never surprises Me? I understand human beings. I thought them up! And I understand sin. That is why I have made flawless provision for it. That provision is the blood of My own Son, Jesus Christ. His part was painful and costly so that your part could be simple. Your part is to repent.

To repent is not to sit around being morosely sorry about what you've done—though you probably will feel sorry. To repent is not to mope around, beating yourself up for your failure—though you may feel that you deserve it. To repent simply means "to turn around." It is a decision word, an action word, not a feeling word. YOUR FEELINGS CAN'T HELP YOU NOW; IT'S TIME TO ACT.

Repent. Turn around. Change your heart and life. Confess, be forgiven, and come home. Do it now!

I'm waiting . . .
God

Pull the Root of Bitterness

Pursue peace with everyone, and holiness—without it no one will see the Lord.
See to it that no one falls short of the grace of God
and that no root of bitterness springs up, causing trouble and by it, defiling many.
—Hebrews 12:14-15

When they arrived at the place called The Skull, they crucified Him there,
along with the criminals, one on the right and one on the left. Then Jesus said,
"Father, forgive them, because they do not know what they are doing."
—Luke 23:33-34

Dear Child,

Did someone who should have been a friend turn out to be an enemy? Has your surprise turned to hurt? Has your hurt turned to righteous indignation and your indignation to anger? Can you now feel that anger putting out little roots of bitterness that will dig into the soil of your tender heart and hold tight? LET ME HELP YOU NOW, MY CHILD. For bitterness will not only poison your life, but it will ruin many other people. Whatever pain you are in, however much you feel you have been wronged, pull up the bitter root before it takes over and spoils the spiritual climate of your whole life

My Son stands beside you. He lives within you. More than anyone, He understands what it is like to be betrayed, denied, mocked, and wronged. And yet, listen to His haunting words. Let them echo down the caverns of your pain: "Father, forgive them, because they do not know what they are doing."

Can you say these words in your situation? Only My Son can give you the grace and the power to do so.

Let Him do it.

God

YOUR THOUGHTS ARE VALUABLE

We demolish arguments and every high-minded thing that is raised up against
the knowledge of God, taking every thought captive to the obedience of Christ.
—2 Corinthians 10:4-5

Take the helmet of salvation, and the sword of the Spirit,
which is God's word.
—Ephesians 6:17

Dearest Child,

Your thoughts are valuable, for they determine to a great degree what your actions will be. My enemy is constantly fighting to gain control in your life, and his first line of attack is always your mind.

BUT YOU ARE NOT TO FEAR, FOR THE VICTORY IS MINE. I have given you every protection you will need. I have placed upon your head a special helmet that protects your mind and its every thought. It is called "the helmet of salvation" because it covers every thought in your mind with the protective reality of your standing in My kingdom. Now, when the enemy's lies begin to fly like arrows, you will recognize them for what they are. Your thoughts will abide in the truth of My Word, and your mind will rest in the reality of who you are in Christ.

You are a sinner saved by grace. You are My precious child. Your knowledge of this truth will allow you to "take every thought captive to the obedience of Christ."

As your thoughts become more Christlike, they will lead you to act with mercy and compassion and wisdom, just as Christ would. As your mind embraces My truth, you will become like My Son.

Think on Him and His love.
God

I HAVE EQUIPPED YOU FULLY

But I protested, "Oh no, Lord GOD! Look,
I don't know how to speak since I am only a youth."
Then the LORD said to me:
Do not say: I am only a youth,
for you will go to everyone I send you to
and speak whatever I tell you.
Do not be afraid of anyone,
for I will be with you to deliver you.
This is the Lord's declaration.

—Jeremiah 1:6-8

My Child,

I can see that you are struggling with feelings of inadequacy. You are not feeling equipped to do all that you must do today. I'm asking you to remember this one thing when the circumstances of your day threaten to discourage you. Remember that I will never ask you to do anything for which I have not first equipped you. You can trust Me on that! You can step out, fully confident, knowing that I am with you. Don't be afraid or intimidated by the people who oppose you. I, the Lord your God, am with you. I WILL SUPPLY YOUR ADEQUACY.

Faithfully,
God

YOU WILL BE SATISFIED

Blessed are those who hunger
and thirst for righteousness,
because they will be filled.
—Matthew 5:6

He must increase, but I must decrease.
—John 3:30

My Dearest Child,

You are blessed indeed when you are hungry and thirsty for Me, for you will be satisfied; you will be filled. Be thankful when you find yourself yearning for more of Me——more guidance, more courage, more comfort, more company. THE DEEP LONGINGS IN YOUR SPIRIT FOR ME WILL MOST SURELY BE ANSWERED.

Nothing is more compelling to My Holy Spirit than a sincere heart that longs for Me and My righteousness. To "hunger for righteousness" is to yearn for a right relationship with Me. And what is a right relationship? One in which you become so infused by and empowered with My Holy Spirit that you bear the mark of My character to all who know you. This is what it means for you to "decrease" so that I may "increase."

Hunger and thirst for Me.
God

I Mean It for Good

But Joseph said to them, "Don't be afraid. Am I in the place of God?
You planned evil against me; God planned it for good to bring about the present result—
the survival of many people."

—Genesis 50:19-20

Child of Mine,

Have you been accused of a wrong by a friend or a brother? Are you writhing under the sting of that accusation? Have a million rationales for your innocence begun to organize in your mind? If your heart is already becoming cold toward your accuser, stop now before you miss what I have for you in this situation. I mean to bring good out of this for you. All that comes to you can be used for your growth and My glory.

SLOW DOWN NOW. Prayerfully clear your heart of malice and defensiveness. Consider the charge. Strip it of the emotionally charged language and see the bare bones of it. Before you take another breath, be brutally honest before Me. Is there any scrap of truth about the accusation, however small? (Avoid the phrase "yes, but . . .") Remember, you are not responsible for the other person's wrongdoing in the situation. I will hold him or her accountable. You are only responsible for your own wrongdoing.

Whatever you find, confess it——to Me and to your accuser. My forgiveness is here for you. Let Me help you bridge that gap and mend that relationship. Come clean. Be forgiven and at peace. Be reconciled.

Your Father,
God

I Have Glorious Plans for You!

"For I know the plans I have for you"—this is the LORD's declaration—
"plans for your welfare, not for disaster, to give you a future and a hope."
—Jeremiah 29:11

For those He foreknew He also predestined to be conformed to the image of His Son,
so that He would be the firstborn among many brothers.
—Romans 8:29

Dear Child of Mine,

Today the future may look bleak or shadowy to you. But, oh, if you could only see what glorious plans I have for you, you would be rejoicing! These are plans to prosper you and bring you joy, not to hurt you nor humiliate you. ALL THAT I HAVE PLANNED HAS BEEN MOTIVATED BY MY DEEP LOVE FOR YOU.

Do not fret or worry about every little detail of My plans right now. They will not be revealed to you today. But as you trust and walk with Me one step at a time, I will reveal them to you. Each day you will know what you need to know. And this much I can tell you today: the purpose of My plan is that you be shaped and molded into the very image of My Son. That is the high calling of your life. So hold on through the darkness and trust Me. I hold you in the hollow of My hand. Nothing comes to you without passing through the strong right hand of My righteousness. All is well.

Your faithful Father,
God

I Want First Place in Your Life

But everything that was a gain to me, I have considered to be a loss because of Christ.
More than that, I also consider everything to be a loss in view of the surpassing value
of knowing Christ Jesus my Lord. Because of Him I have suffered
the loss of all things and consider them filth, so that I may gain Christ.

—Philippians 3:7-8

Then God spoke all these words:
I am the LORD your God, who brought you out of the land of Egypt,
out of the place of slavery.
Do not have other gods besides Me.

—Exodus 20:1-3

Dear Child,

Of what are you proudest in your life? What brings you the most joy? What really defines who you are? Whatever these things are (family, career, friendships, even service to Me), offer up thanks for them, for they are a gift. And then, gratefully, move them into second place.

Every good thing must come second to the best thing——knowing Me. What you once considered gain, now consider it loss compared to the joy of knowing Me. Whatever was valuable, now consider it trash compared to the joy of walking with Me. I'm speaking of priorities. You should not despise your family, work, or ministry. But knowing Me must mean more to you. For I love you with a jealous love. I will not share first place in your affection with anything. LOVING ME MUST BE THE PASSION THAT DEFINES YOUR LIFE.

What would you answer when asked, "Who are you, and what do you do?" Would you say, "I am a mother," "I am a computer analyst," or "I preach the gospel of Christ"? All of these are second-place answers. Instead, I would have you answer, "I am the beloved child of the most high God, whom I delight to know."

Jealously yours,
God

HERE'S HOW TO SHOW YOUR LOVE

Little children, we must not love in word or speech, but in deed and truth.

—1 John 3:18

Isn't the fast I choose: To break the chains of wickedness,
to untie the ropes of the yoke, to set the oppressed free, and to tear off every yoke?
Is it not to share your bread with the hungry, to bring the poor and homeless into your house,
to clothe the naked when you see him, and to not ignore your own flesh and blood?
Then your light will appear like the dawn, and your recovery will come quickly.
Your righteousness will go before you, and the LORD's glory will be your rear guard.
At that time, when you call, the LORD will answer; when you cry out,
He will say: Here I am....The LORD will always lead you, satisfy you in a parched land,
and strengthen your bones. You will be like a watered garden
and like a spring whose waters never run dry.

—Isaiah 58:6-9, 11

Dear Child,

You have told Me that you love Me, and you long to prove your love. But how? you wonder. What do I desire of you? Will I be impressed with lofty words or fasts or sacrifices? No. Here is the way to show Me your love. Here is the way to My heart. Break the chains of injustice. Stand for the oppressed. Free those around you who are in bondage. Welcome strangers. Share your food with the hungry, and open your home to those who have no place to go. And don't get so busy helping the needy that you forget your own family. Love your wife, your husband, your parents. Listen to your children, and let them know they are important to you. When you do these things, then you will feel My pleasure and share My delight. For your light will break forth like the dawn, and all that is sick in your own soul will be healed. You will call Me, and I will answer. I will continually guide you. I WILL SATISFY YOUR DEEPEST NEEDS AND STRENGTHEN YOU. And you will be like a well-watered garden, like a spring whose waters never fail.

To show your love for Me, love others.
God

COME, BE RENEWED

Do you not know?
Have you not heard?
Yahweh is the everlasting God,
the Creator of the whole earth.
He never grows faint or weary;
there is no limit to His understanding.
He gives strength to the weary and strengthens the powerless.
Youths may faint and grow weary, and young men stumble and fall,
but those who trust in the LORD will renew their strength;
they will soar on wings like eagles;
they will run and not grow weary;
they will walk and not faint.

—Isaiah 40:28-31

My Precious One,

The world you live in is obsessed with staying young. Every day you see people around you spending enormous amounts of time and energy and money on any scheme that promises to keep them youthful. Some have mastered the art of looking young on the outside while their spirits within them are withered and old. They are tired of the uphill struggle of their existence and bored with its routines; they hunger for something more. Above the roar and the rumble of their stressful lives I am calling them, saying, "Do you not know? Have you not heard? I am the Lord, the everlasting God, the Creator of the whole earth. I give strength to the weary and power to the weak. Everyone who chases the world's vain pursuits will grow weary and old. BUT THOSE WHO TRUST IN ME WILL RENEW THEIR STRENGTH. They will soar like eagles. They will run and not grow weary. They will walk without growing tired."

Come to Me and be renewed.
God

SOMEONE UNDERSTANDS

Therefore since we have a great high priest who has passed through the heavens—
Jesus the Son of God—let us hold fast to the confession.
For we do not have a high priest who is unable to sympathize with our weaknesses,
but One who has been tested in every way as we are, yet without sin.
Therefore let us approach the throne of grace with boldness,
so that we may receive mercy and find grace to help us at the proper time.
—Hebrews 4:14-16

Who is the one who condemns?
Christ Jesus is the One who died, but even more, has been raised;
He also is at the right hand of God and intercedes for us.
—Romans 8:34

My Child,

Sometimes you feel that no one understands what you are going through. Even those closest to you don't seem to comprehend or care. I want you to know today that you are not alone. For I have given you more than a Savior, more than a distant and ethereal high priest who exists above all human experience. I HAVE GIVEN YOU A FRIEND WHO HAS WALKED THROUGH THIS HUMAN LIFE BEFORE YOU.

How well He understands your breaking heart! How well He knows what it is to be beaten back by fatigue, plagued by enemies, misunderstood by friends. Whatever you are struggling with today, He has struggled with that same emotion or feeling. Whatever your temptation, He was tempted that way, too. Wherever your feet are on the journey, His footprints are in the road ahead of you.

Never again do I want you to say that no one understands. Jesus Christ understands, and because He sits at My right hand day and night interceding for you, I am constantly being reminded of your plight. I encourage you, My child, to come into My presence with boldness and confidence. Tell Me what's going on. I have mercy for your sins and grace to uplift you when you're hurting.

You see, I understand, too.
God

OPEN YOUR CLENCHED FISTS

Yours, LORD, is the greatness and the power and the glory

and the splendor and the majesty,

for everything in the heavens and on earth belongs to You.

Yours, LORD, is the kingdom, and You are exalted as head over all.

Riches and honor come from You, and You are the ruler of everything.

In Your hand are power and might,

and it is in Your hand to make great and give strength to all.

—1 Chronicles 29:11-12

The earth and everything in it, the world and its inhabitants,

belong to the LORD.

—Psalm 24:1

Dear Child of Mine,

You take great pride in your ownership of certain things. You fret over your money and how you will spend it, your work and how you will be compensated for it, your possessions and how to protect them. How much more peaceful you will be once you have come to the realization that everything you "own" is really owned by Me. All that you "possess" is actually on loan to you for a season. Your things, your money, your family, your job, even the gifts and talents that allow you to do your job—all of these are Mine.

I have given you stewardship over these things for a time. Enjoy them. Be thankful for them. Use them well. But do not worry over them, for they are My concern. You can trust them to my care.

So as you dress for work tomorrow morning, think how best you can honor Me as you go to My job! As you write a check, ask Me how I would have you disperse My money! As you pray for your family, say, "Father, these loved ones of mine are really Yours." Open your clenched fists and PUT THE CONTROL OF YOUR LIFE AND YOUR POSSESSIONS BACK WHERE IT BELONGS. In My hands.

Trust Me.
God

ALWAYS BE THANKFUL!

Rejoice always! Pray constantly. Give thanks in everything,
for this is God's will for you in Christ Jesus.
—1 Thessalonians 5:16-18

Dear Child,

When good things come into your life, come to Me and give thanks. When financial and material blessings come to you, give thanks. When you wake on an autumn morning, and the air is cool and filled with promise, and your eyes are amazed by the awesome beauty of My creation, give thanks to Me. When your loved ones are gathered close and your heart is filled with the joy of their company, give Me thanks.

But when trouble comes, when questions crowd your mind, when those close to you have let you down, when the skies turn dark and help seems far away——what then?

Then, too, give Me thanks. Know that I am in control. Thank Me, knowing that in spite of what you see with your eyes, I am working My will in every situation. That I have promised never to leave you nor forsake you. That I love you and am very near——nearer than your tears and nearer than your trouble.

In good times, your thanks will flow from a heart of gratitude. In difficult times, your thanks will flow from a heart of faith. BUT AT ALL TIMES, GIVE ME THANKS.

Your faithful provider,
God

THIS IS A JOB FOR YOU

The Spirit of the Lord GOD is on Me,
because the LORD has anointed Me
to bring good news to the poor.
He has sent Me to heal the brokenhearted,
to proclaim liberty to the captives,
and freedom to the prisoners.

—Isaiah 61:1

My Child,

I have given you a huge and amazing job. You may say, "Lord, how can I do all that? I'm just one person!" Don't you think I realize that? Of course I do. BUT I NEVER GIVE A JOB TO A CHILD OF MINE WITHOUT FIRST EQUIPPING THAT CHILD TO DO THE JOB. So let's look at what I've asked you to do.

Preach good news to the poor. "I'm not a preacher," you may say. But everyone can preach good news by the way he lives. Does your life speak good news? Can people whose spirits are poor look at you and say, "This world must be a great and joyful place," just by what they see in your life? Does your friendship bind up the brokenhearted? Is your love proclaiming freedom to those who are captive to the world's addictions: money, drugs, the approval of others? Is your friendship bringing light to those who have no light?

It's not that complicated. It's not that super-religious. It's you loving others for Me. They're all around you. Can you do it for Me? I know you can do it if you will. Will you?

The Sovereign Lord,
God

YOUR WORK IS NOT MY FIRST CONCERN

Don't you believe that I am in the Father and the Father is in Me?

The words I speak to you I do not speak on My own.

The Father who lives in Me does His works.

Believe Me that I am in the Father and Father is in Me.

Otherwise, believe because of the works themselves.

I assure you: The one who believes in Me will also do the works that I do.

And he will do even greater works than these, because I am going to the Father.

—John 14:10-12

Dear Child,

I watch you laboring and fretting and anxiously striving to achieve things for Me and My kingdom. Hear Me. Your work is not My primary concern. YOUR WORK IS NOW, HAS ALWAYS BEEN, AND ALWAYS WILL BE SECONDARY TO YOUR RELATIONSHIP WITH ME.

What you do will flow out of your relationship with Me as irrigation streams flow out of a deep, clear, powerful river. The river (the relationship) will set your motives and supply your strength. Then your work will flow forth to honor Me. Any time you allow your work to come ahead of your relationship with Me, you risk working against Me and My purposes.

Draw near to Me and rest. Seek My will at every small turn. Listen for My voice. Be filled with My Spirit. Then work with joy and abandon!

The source of your power,
God

GET A GRIP! STAND STEADY

For they disciplined us for a short time based on what seemed good to them,
but He does it for our benefit, so that we can share His holiness.
No discipline seems enjoyable at the time, but painful.
Later on, however, it yields the fruit of peace and righteousness
to those who have been trained by it.
Therefore strengthen your tired hands and weakened knees,
and make straight paths for your feet,
so that what is lame may not be dislocated, but healed instead.
—Hebrews 12:10-13

My Child,

Someday you'll look back at what you're going through now with a different perspective. Every adult who has come out of a loving home can remember trying times in the past. Nobody's childhood is all fun and games. At some point the ideas of the child and the ideas of the parent will be in conflict. But a parent who operates out of love is strong enough to make the hard calls, whether or not they make us happy at the time.

THE IMPORTANT THING IS THE ULTIMATE RESULT. What kind of adult is this child going to become? Though the discipline of our youth is never pleasant, in retrospect we are often able to see what it was about. This will be true in your spiritual life as well. When My purposes are accomplished, you will look back at these tedious and painful times and see what I was doing in your life. If you accept this time prayerfully and obediently, you will be able to watch the fruit of real goodness grow up in you because of it.

So get a grip! Stand steady! Don't wander off, but stay close to Me and forge ahead! The foot that stays on the right path will not stumble.

I love you!
God

SPEAK A BLESSING TO SOMEONE

The words that I have spoken to you are spirit and are life.
—John 6:63b

Either make the tree good and its fruit good, or make the tree bad and its fruit bad;
for a tree is known by its fruit. Brood of vipers!
How can you speak good things when you are evil?
For the mouth speaks from the overflow of the heart.
A good man produces good things from his storeroom of good,
and an evil man produces evil things from his storeroom of evil.
—Matthew 12:33-35

Dearest Child,

Pay attention to the words you speak today. Your words are the evidence of your heart, for the mouth speaks the things that are in the heart. As the fruit of a tree tells what kind of tree it is, your words will tell what kind of person you are inside. Whatever you have stored up in your secret self will be revealed by what you are saying to those around you. Your words have the power to crush or restore, to tear down or build up, to demoralize or encourage. When you are filled to overflowing with My Holy Spirit, your words cannot help but be a blessing to others. Jesus said, "The words that I have spoken to you are spirit and are life." DWELL ON HIS WORDS SO THAT THE WORDS WHICH OVERFLOW FROM YOU MAY ALSO BE LIFE-GIVING. Speak a blessing to someone today.

Your Father,
God

BRING ME THE THINGS THAT WORRY YOU

At that time Jesus said, "I praise You, Father, Lord of heaven and earth,
because You have hidden these things from the wise and learned and revealed them to infants.
Yes, Father, because this was Your good pleasure.
All things have been entrusted to Me by My Father.
No one knows the Son except the Father, and no one knows the Father except the Son
and anyone to whom the Son desires to reveal Him.
Come to Me, all of you who are weary and burdened, and I will give you rest.
All of you, take up My yoke and learn from Me, because I am gentle and humble in heart,
and you will find rest for yourselves. For My yoke is easy and My burden is light."

—Matthew 11:25-30

Dear Child,

I have hidden the treasures of My heart from the worldly-wise and cynical, but I am revealing them now to you, for I see that you are willing to humble yourself and come to Me like a child. What pleasure you give Me when you are simple and trusting and childlike! Then, more than ever, I delight in you.

I am known to no one but My Son and those to whom He chooses to reveal My nature. When your heart is open to Him, My heart is open to you!

Come now, bringing the things that worry or trouble you, the things that produce stress in your life. I did not create you to bear these things in your human strength. If you let Me, I will carry them.

YOU HAVE MUCH TO LEARN FROM JESUS. Spend time with Him. You will find that His yoke is easy and His burden is light. This is the kind of load you are created to carry. Put on His gentleness and humility, and enter into My rest.

Come!
God

WHY DO YOU QUESTION MY DESIGN?

Woe to the one who argues with his Maker—

one clay pot among many.

Does clay say to the one forming it:

What are you making?

Or does your work say:

He has no hands?

—Isaiah 45:9

Dear Child of Mine,

There are still some things about yourself that you have not accepted. You view your abilities and assets with harsh and critical eyes and keep a constant record of your "limitations." You murmur and say, "I was made this way, but I should have been made that way!" or "If only I could be like this person or that person!"

Why do you insist on being your own worst enemy? Why do you question the judgment of the God who made you as you are? Does the clay say to the potter, "What are you doing? How dare you shape Me this way?" No, the clay does not give advice to the potter. And neither are you to resist My design for your life.

I, YOUR GOD AND YOUR CREATOR, HAVE FASHIONED YOU FOR MY PURPOSES. Humble your heart. Embrace My way. Give thanks.

Your own
God

COME FORTH AND LIVE!

The hand of the LORD was on me, and He brought me out by His Spirit
and set me down in the middle of the valley: it was full of bones....
He said to me, "Prophesy concerning these bones and say to them:
Dry bones, hear the word of the LORD! This is what the Lord GOD says to these bones:
I will cause breath to enter you, and you will live .... Then you will know that I am the LORD."
So I prophesied as I had been commanded. While I was prophesying, there was a noise,
a rattling sound, and the bones came together, bone to bone....
the breath entered them, and they came to life and stood on their feet, a vast army.
Then He said to me ... "I will put My Spirit in you, and you will live, and I will settle you
in your own land. Then you will know that I am the LORD. I have spoken, and I will do it."
—Ezekiel 37:1-14

He redeems your life from the Pit; He crowns you with faithful love and compassion.
—Psalm 103:4

My Own Child,

Are you going through a dry, desert time? Has your hope evaporated? Do you feel cut off from Me and from others? Does your spirit feel more dead than alive? Listen to Me now, My child. On your own you have no power to revive yourself——no power to bring life. But what you do have is the power to choose. You can choose today to call upon My name. You can choose to receive a new beginning from My hand. WHEN YOU CALL, I WILL HEAR YOU.

I will open the grave of your despair. I will bring you back to the land of living. And then you will know that I am the Lord, the God who rescues you from the grave. I will put My Spirit in you, and you will live. I will settle you in the land of your spiritual inheritance. And you will bear testimony to all who ask that I, the Lord your God, have done it!

Come forth and live!
God

PRAISING ME CAN HEAL YOU

My soul, praise the LORD, and all that is within me, praise His holy name....

Do not forget all His benefits.

He forgives all your sin; He heals all your diseases....

He satisfies you with goodness; your youth is renewed like the eagle....

The LORD is compassionate and gracious, slow to anger and full of faithful love....

As far as the east is from the west, so far has He removed our transgressions from us....

From eternity to eternity the Lord's faithful love is toward those who fear Him.

—Psalm 103:1-17

My Dear Child,

Did you know that praising Me can heal you? It can still your restless spirit and fill your empty soul. TURN TO ME AND BRING ME PRAISE. Let it spring from deep within your inmost being. Let your song exalt My holy name.

   Remember My mercies and all of My benefits, for I am the God who heals and forgives. I am the Father who redeems your life and satisfies you with good things. I make you young again, like the eagle. Praise Me, for I am slow to anger and abounding in love. I remove your sins as far from you as the east is from the west. Praise Me, for My love continues forever. Turn to Me and bring Me praise.

I am the Lord, your
God

COME AWAY FROM THE COMFORTABLE

As He was walking along the Sea of Galilee, He saw two brothers,
Simon, who was called Peter, and his brother Andrew.
They were casting a net into the sea, since they were fishermen.
"Follow Me," He told them, "and I will make you fish for people."
Immediately they left their nets and followed Him.
—Matthew 4:18-20

A scribe approached Him and said, "Teacher, I will follow You wherever You go!"
Jesus told him, "Foxes have dens and birds of the sky have nests,
but the Son of Man has no place to lay His head."
—Matthew 8:19-20

When Jesus heard this, He told him, "You still lack one thing: sell all that you have
and distribute it to the poor, and you will have treasure in heaven. Then come, follow Me."
After he heard this, he became extremely sad, because he was very rich.
—Luke 18:22-23

My Child,

Are you fashioning for yourself a life of comfort——a place where you can run away from reality?

Listen. Do you hear it? Somewhere on the margins of your comfort zone there is a voice crying out to you——a voice too persistent to ignore.

"Follow Me," it keeps saying. "Follow Me. Come away from the safe and the comfortable, the predictable and the socially correct. Follow Me into a life of risk and challenge and high adventure, where the cost will be great but the rewards will be greater. Follow Me, and I will make your existence count for more than comfort. I will lead you on narrow paths, up steep and rugged roads, into dangerous terrain. But I will give you weapons for the battle. I WILL FIGHT BESIDE YOU. And you will share My victory!"

Come away and follow!
God

YOU ARE A PORTRAIT IN PROGRESS

We all, with unveiled faces, are reflecting the glory of the Lord
and are being transformed into the same image from glory to glory;
this is from the Lord who is the Spirit.

—2 Corinthians 3:18

Dearest Child,

I AM CONSTANTLY WORKING IN YOUR LIFE——adding this color, that shadow, this line. Like an artist with a paintbrush, I am making you into the very image of My beautiful and sinless Son.

Don't constantly question what I am doing. Don't struggle against My hand. Learn to trust the Artist who stands back and sees from his own perspective what is needed in the portrait he is creating.

If you must question something today, ask this: "How will the circumstances of this day make me more like Jesus?" Then thank Me for those circumstances and receive My grace to walk through them. I love you with a tenderness you cannot imagine.

Your Abba,
God

RETURN TO ME

The word of the LORD came to me:
"Go and announce directly to Jerusalem that this is what the LORD says:
I remember the loyalty of your youth,
your love as a bride—
how you followed Me in the wilderness,
in a land not sown."
—Jeremiah 2:1-2

Dear Child of Mine,

I remember the excitement of your early faith——the way you loved Me, the way you followed so trustingly as I led you to the other side of that "desert time" you were going through. Always your first thoughts were of Me. I was never far from your heart back then. You gave Me the first fruits of your time, your energy, your attention. YOU NEEDED ME, AND I WAS THERE FOR YOU.

Where are you today? I haven't moved. I am still here, longing to spend time with you.

Your loving Father,
God

CRY OUT TO ME

So [the blind man] called out, "Jesus, Son of David, have mercy on me!"

Then those in front told him to keep quiet, but he kept crying out all the more,

"Son of David, have mercy on me!"

Jesus stopped and commanded that he be brought to Him.

When he drew near, He asked him "What do you want Me to do for you?"

"Lord" he said, "I want to see!"

"Receive your sight!" Jesus told him. "Your faith has healed you."

—Luke 18:38-42

My Child,

Cry out to Me. Ask Me what you will. Do not let others discourage you or dissuade you from seeking what you need from Me. Be specific. Tell Me exactly what you want Me to do for you. And ask in the name of Jesus, My Son. (To ask in His name means to ask in accordance with His nature. I will not hear or respond to a request that is contrary to the nature of My incarnate Word, My Son.) Ask believing. Don't put your faith in faith, for faith in and of itself cannot help you. Instead put your faith in Me— in My willingness to heal and My power to change things.

Cry out boldly. Ask specifically. Use the name of Jesus. HAVE FAITH IN ME. And like the blind man of Jericho, you will receive what you need.

Mercifully,
God

THE NEWS IS GOOD

Blessed be the God and Father of our Lord Jesus Christ,

who has blessed us with every spiritual blessing in the heavens, in Christ;

for He chose us in Him, before the foundation of the world,

to be holy and blameless in His sight.

In love He predestined us to be adopted through Jesus Christ for Himself,

according to His favor and will, to the praise of His glorious grace

that He favored us with in the Beloved.

In Him we have redemption through His blood, the forgiveness of our trespasses,

according to the riches of His grace that He lavished on us

with all wisdom and understanding.

He made known to us the mystery of His will, according to His good pleasure

that He planned in Him for the administration of the days of fulfillment—

to bring everything together in the Messiah, both things in heaven and things on earth in Him.

—Ephesians 1:3-10

My Dear Child,

Could you use a little good news today? Could you use a lot? Then know these things: I have blessed you with every spiritual blessing in the person of Jesus, My Son. I have held nothing back!

Every spiritual blessing I possess is yours, in Him. Long before I even created the world, you were the one I wanted, the one I chose, to be holy—set apart for Me! I knew way back then that I wanted you for My child. This was My pleasure. I desired to pour out on you all the grace I possess. And I did that very thing when I gave you My Son as your Savior, your advocate, your friend. IN JESUS YOU HAVE EVERYTHING! Freedom through His blood. Forgiveness of sins. Full wisdom and understanding.

I've even revealed to you the mystery of My will: I am going to bring everything in heaven and earth together under one head, Jesus Christ. No more separation or sadness. Everything will be united in Him.

When the stress of your day starts getting to you, think about this. The news is good. Very good.

Your Creator and King,
God

Now You Belong

So then, remember that at one time you were Gentiles in the flesh—
called "the uncircumcised" by those called "the circumcised," done by hand in the flesh.
At that time you were without the Messiah, excluded from the citizenship of Israel,
and foreigners to the covenants of the promise, with no hope and without God in the world.
But now in Christ Jesus, you who were far away
have been brought near by the blood of the Messiah.
—Ephesians 2:11-13

My Own,

Once you were on the outside, looking in. You were like a child whose nose is pressed against the window of a beautiful shop full of toys and candy, with no money to buy. You are like a child on the playground who longs to take part in the game but never gets picked to be on a team. You were like the foreigner who can't understand the language or traditions of the strange land he is traveling through. How lonely and lost he feels!

But now everything has changed. My son has come for you. Now you belong; you are a part; you are on the inside! Jesus Christ has opened the door to the beautiful shop and has paid the price for your purchases. Jesus Christ has stopped the game and come over to you on the sidelines and has chosen you to be on His team. Jesus Christ has welcomed you into a new land where He is the king. He has taught you the language and the customs and made you a citizen. NOW, AT LAST, YOU ARE A MEMBER OF THE HOUSEHOLD OF GOD!

Welcome, My child!
God

THE ENDING IS GOOD

He will wipe away every tear from their eyes.
Death will exist no longer;
grief, crying, and pain will exist no longer,
because the previous things have passed away.

—Revelation 21:4

My Dear Child,

Do you ever wish you could ask Me face-to-face why everyone on earth seems to be having so many problems? Or what about wars? Or crime? Or diseases? I know how troubling all of those things can be to you. It's like wanting to turn to the back of the novel and read the last chapter to find out how it all comes out. I want you to trust Me when I tell you that the ending is good. IT'S NOT JUST GOOD. IT'S PERFECT IN EVERY WAY, MY CHILD.

Every question that you have ever had on this earth will be answered. Every tear that you have cried on this earth will be dried. You and I and all of My people will be together in a place of beauty and glory and wonder and perfection forever and ever, where there will be no more death or mourning or crying or pain, for the old will pass away and I will make all things new.

The Alpha and the Omega,
God

BEGIN IN YOUR HEART

Woe to you, scribes and Pharisees, hypocrites!
You are like whitewashed tombs, which appear beautiful on the outside,
but inside are full of dead men's bones and every impurity.
In the same way, on the outside you seem righteous to people,
but inside you are full of hypocrisy and lawlessness.
—Matthew 23:27-28

My Dear Child,

When you bend all of your energy toward doing what is right and behaving as a good Christian should, the strain of your efforts will eventually show in your disposition. You will find yourself growing short-tempered with others——impatient with their flaws and errors. You will judge as less worthy than yourself anyone who seems less involved in striving for right behavior. And before you know it, your inner attitude will be saturated with the poison of pride.

This is exactly what happened to the Pharisees. They got so carried away with the rigid rules of external behavior that their hearts got far from Me. On the outside, to the people on the street, they looked like perfection itself. But on the inside, where only I could see, they were filled with the rottenness of self-consciousness and pride. So don't begin with the outer you, striving to do holy things. Instead, begin in your heart by confessing that, apart from Me, you are unable to be holy. Humbly lay down your own efforts at being "a good person" and let My Spirit fill you with My holiness, My goodness, My love.

You are so precious to Me. I WANT TO FILL YOU WITH NEW LIFE.

Your loving Father,
God

USE WHAT IS YOURS!

I pray that the eyes of your heart may be enlightened
so you may know what is the hope of His calling,
what are the glorious riches of His inheritance among the saints,
and what is the immeasurable greatness of His power to us who believe,
according to the working of His vast strength.
He demonstrated this power in the Messiah by raising Him from the dead
and seating Him at His right hand in the heavens.

—Ephesians 1:18-20

Dearest Child of Mine,

If your banker called to tell you that someone had died and left you millions of dollars, how long would it take you to get dressed and down to the bank? You wouldn't leave the money there unclaimed and never write a single check on it, would you? Well, I am telling you today that you have an inheritance worth far more than millions of dollars. It has already been deposited to your account——yet you are not using it.

What is your inheritance? I have deposited to your spiritual account an unlimited supply of power. What kind of power? The exact same power that raised My Son Jesus Christ from the dead! The exact same power that seated Him at My right hand here in heaven, high above all earthly rule, authority, power, or dominion! THAT IS THE KIND OF POWER THAT BELONGS TO YOU WHEN YOU BELIEVE IN HIM.

Why do you sometimes go around with the attitude of a spiritual pauper? It is time to use what is yours. It is time to spend your inheritance for the spread of My kingdom.

Powerfully,
God

THANK ME FOR TRIALS

Consider it a great joy, my brothers, whenever you experience various trials,
knowing that the testing of your faith produces endurance.
But endurance must do its complete work,
so that you may be mature and complete, lacking nothing.

—James 1:2-4

Dear Child,

You may have thought that once you became a Christian all temptations and trials would disappear. Not so. Even Jesus was tempted, and He endured terrible trials. Temptations and trials are a part of your life while you are on this earth. THEY ARE ALSO PART OF MY PLAN FOR YOU. They force you to lean into My mercy and rely on My power. So don't resent them as enemies, but welcome them as friends! As they test your faith, they produce in you a valuable quality: endurance. And as this endurance becomes strong within you, you will find that you have gained the kind of spiritual maturity you never thought was possible—and all because of your trials and temptations. Thank Me today for those trials and temptations, and trust Me to overcome them in you through the power of My Holy Spirit!

Your Deliverer,
God

COME BELIEVING

Then Jesus said to him, "'If You can?' Everything is possible to the one who believes."

Immediately the father of the boy cried out, "I do believe! Help my unbelief."

—Mark 9:23-24

Now if any of you lacks wisdom, he should ask God,

who gives to all generously and without criticizing, and it will be given to him.

But let him ask in faith without doubting.

For the doubter is like the surging sea, driven and tossed by the wind.

That person should not expect to receive anything from the Lord.

An indecisive man is unstable in all his ways.

—James 1:5-8

My Dear Child,

When you need wisdom, come to Me. I will supply it generously. But when you come, come believing, not doubting. The tiniest doubt splits the sails on your vessel of faith.

How do you handle the doubts that plague you? First of all, don't pretend. Be forthright with Me. If you do have doubts, you cannot hide them from Me, for I know you. Shine a flashlight on each small doubt that creeps, as an intruder, into your heart. Then ask Me for help—for more faith. I will supply that, too. LEARN TO PRAY LIKE THIS: "I DO BELIEVE! HELP MY UNBELIEF!"

There is no need to be tentative or shaky. I am your God. I know your heart and can heal your doubts. I supply faith and wisdom and guidance at every crossroads in your life.

Come believing!
God

SHARE WHAT YOU HAVE BEEN GIVEN

Blessed be the God and Father of our Lord Jesus Christ,
the Father of mercies and the God of all comfort.
He comforts us in all our affliction, so that we may be able
to comfort those who are in any kind of affliction,
through the comfort we ourselves receive from God.
For as the sufferings of Christ overflow to us,
so our comfort overflows through Christ.

—2 Corinthians 1:3-5

Child of My Kingdom,

There is someone very near you today who needs to know what you know. Someone who needs a word of comfort or compassion or encouragement.

When you were low, did someone lift you? When you were lost, did someone help you find the way? I allowed these difficult times in your life so you could experience My mercy. And now someone else is going through a difficult time. Will you be the one to bring My mercy, to share My comfort and guidance? Will you spread the light of My truth as one small candle spreads its light to another?

In this world, you are either part of the problem or part of the solution—part of the darkness or part of the light. When you were engulfed in problems, someone brought My merciful solution to you. When you had doubts and questions, someone answered your questions with My healing and life-changing truth. Now it is time for you to share what you have been given with someone in need. WILL YOU REACH OUT TO SOMEONE TODAY . . . FOR ME?

Share My love.
God

Books by Claire Cloninger

from New Hope Publishers

KALEIDOSCOPE

WHEN THE GLASS SLIPPER DOESN'T FIT

(coauthored with Karla Worley)